ME AND MY PONY

The Big Event

Toni Webber

FRANKLIN WATTS
London · Sydney

Produced by:
Aladdin Books Ltd
28 Percy Street
London W1T 2BZ

ISBN 0-7496-4490-7

*First published in Great Britain
in 2002 by:*
Franklin Watts
96 Leonard Street
London EC2A 4XD

Editor:
Harriet Brown

Designers:
Flick, Book Design & Graphics
Simon Morse

Illustrators:
Terry Riley, Simon Morse

Cartoons: Simon Morse

Certain illustrations have
appeared in earlier books
created by Aladdin Books.

Printed in UAE

A CIP catalogue record for
this book is available from
the British Library.

Contents

Introduction

The Big Event is a lively guide to entering competitions with your pony. Once you have mastered the basics of riding, there is likely to be a time when you start to think about competing. There are many activities you can try with your pony, from showing to dressage to gymkhana games. Most shows cater for all abilities, so you will always be competing against riders of a similar standard to you. You never know, you might just win a rosette or two.

Competing sounds so exciting! I'd love to win a rosette. Mind you, it looks like fun whether you win or not.

Always remember to...

...look in these boxes for further information about competing with your pony. They contain important points that you should try to remember.

THE RIGHTS AND WRONGS

Look out for these tick boxes. They show you how to do things properly. Just as importantly, look out for the cross boxes. These show you how not to do things.

Q What are these boxes for?

A These question and answer panels are here to help answer your questions about any aspect of competing. Each panel is relevant to the subject on the rest of the page.

Wednesday
I was talking to my friends at the stables today. They were telling me that going in for competitions is their favourite way to spend the school holidays. The owner of our stables even lets people hire her ponies to enter shows.

Entering competitions

It is not the winning but the taking part that makes competing so much fun. Training your pony to meet certain standards or to tackle a difficult jumping course is very satisfying. Of course, if you are placed, or better still, come first, that's a big bonus.

FIND OUT WHAT'S ON

Most organisers advertise their events in a local newspaper. Events usually fall into one of three categories – horse shows, hunter trials or one-day events. Horse shows are a mixture of showing, jumping and gymkhana games. Hunter trials are a cross-country competition, and one-day events include dressage, show jumping and cross-country.

WHAT TO ENTER

First you need to get a schedule from the organisers of the classes that are going to be held. Look carefully at the classes to see which ones suit you best. A nice-looking, reliable pony that is a steady jumper may be well suited to a Working Hunter Pony class. Show jumping is a good choice if your pony is quick, agile and doesn't knock down fences too often. Most ponies enjoy cross-country, which involves jumping solid jumps, ditches and sometimes water. All-round ponies suit the Best Pony Club Pony class and you can enter old ponies in the Veteran class. Little, nippy ponies are often good at gymkhana games, especially if you are as active as they are. Check the timing of the classes (see page 8).

Tuesday
I'm going to enter lots of shows this season. My friend Annabel says that Oscar should do the Working Hunter Pony class because he's such a safe jumper. He hardly ever knocks down any fences.

FILL IN THE FORM

Every schedule should come with an entry form. You must fill in the classes you want to enter, your name and your pony's name, your age and the name of the pony's owner. More than one pony or rider can be entered on the same form. Make sure that the cheque is completed and return it with the form to the organiser before the closing date.

Horse show
12 years and under show - Saturday 9th September
Entry form

Class No.	Name of horse/pony	Name of rider	Age	Owner	Entry fee
6	Bobby Sox	Hermione Russell	9	Rider	xx
9	Bobby Sox	Cressida May	8	H. Russell	xx
12	Hannibal	Henry Russell	7	Rider	xx
13	Hannibal	Henry Russell	7	Rider	xx
				Red Cross	£xx per rider
				Total	£xx

Entries close: Tuesday 5th September
Cheques payable to: Southdown Hunt East Pony Club

Name...... **H. Russell** .....Tel. No...**01234 5678913**

Address...**1 The Drive, South London**

Entries to: Miss A. Person, 10 The Road, The Green, Townsville

Always remember to...

...keep your pony interested in what it is doing. Practice makes perfect, but not if you jump the same jump over and over again. Even the happiest pony will get bored and start refusing. Try to think of exciting things for your pony to do. For example, when out hacking, jump fallen logs to add variety to your ride. It is also a good idea to ride through small streams to get your pony used to water.

PONY FITNESS

If your pony is ridden regularly and is on the right diet, getting and keeping it fit should not be difficult. Walking and trotting up and down hills will help to build up muscle. Regular schooling will teach your pony to be obedient and help to make it flexible and responsive to your commands. If possible, have lessons with an experienced instructor. This stops bad habits from developing. If you are expecting your pony to do more exercise than usual, you may have to adjust its diet. Ask an experienced person to help you work out the right amount to feed your pony.

4 pm – I made a really good job of plaiting Oscar's mane once I got the hang of it. I only had to redo two plaits, so I was quite pleased. I did them the night before the show and covered them with some old nylon tights to keep them tidy.

Getting ready

The secret of having a good time at a show is one word – preparation. If you allow enough time to get both yourself and your pony ready, you will arrive at the show in the right state of mind. Here's how you do it...

Sponges

Q What grooming kit do I need to take with me?

A If you are entering a showing class, you will need a body brush, stable rubber, hoof pick and hoof oil. You will also need sponges to wipe round your pony's eyes, nostrils and dock area (under its tail). In a cross-country competition, it helps to have a water carrier and bucket, together with a large sponge, for sponging your pony down.

Hoof pick

Body brush

Q What other preparations do I need?

A It sounds obvious, but if possible, try to get a good night's sleep the night before a show. It is easy to be so excited about the following day that sleep won't come. Go to bed at your normal time, take a warm drink, have a hot bath (anything that makes you relax), set the alarm and go to sleep. You will have a far better time if you are wide awake and thinking clearly for the competition.

GROOMING

Grooming for a show is not very different from the grooming you give your pony every day. Any light-coloured hair on your pony, such as its socks (white markings on its legs), may need special care to remove grass stains. You can use powdered chalk as extra whitening.

Sew up plait.

Bunch plait.

PLAITING THE MANE AND TAIL

Divide the well-brushed mane into evenly sized bunches. Tightly plait each bunch. Use a needle and thread to sew up the end (step 1, left). Turn the end under, roll it up and stitch it firmly in place (step 2, left). For the tail, plait it from the top, drawing in hairs evenly from each side (right). Before you reach the end of the tail bone, stop drawing in side hairs and make a thin plait the length of the tail. Tuck it under to form a loop and stitch it in place.

CLEANING TACK

If you are going to clean your tack properly, you must take it to pieces. So it is important that you learn how to put it together again first. Wash all the metal work in soapy water. Rinse it well and dry thoroughly. If the leatherwork is muddy, remove mud with a damp cloth. Rub saddle soap into the leather with a slightly damp sponge. If there is any foam at all, your sponge is too wet. You can put your numnah (the cloth that goes under the saddle) and cloth girth in the washing machine. Leather girths should be saddle-soaped.

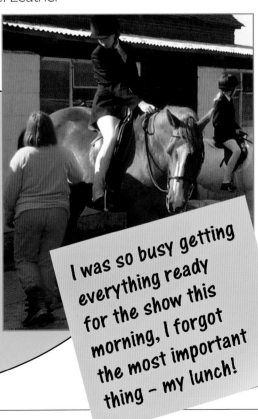

Always remember to...

...get everything ready the night before. You do not want to have to hunt for anything just when you should calmly be eating your breakfast. Clean your jodhpur boots, brush your jacket and hat and check that you have a clean shirt the night before the show. Have you got two riding gloves or is one still somewhere at the back of the wardrobe, where you chucked it last time you wore it? You will still have to clean your pony, so it may help to pack all your show clothes into a holdall and take them with you to the stables. Then you can change into them once your pony is ready. Don't forget to put some money in your pocket, as well as a clean handkerchief.

I was so busy getting everything ready for the show this morning, I forgot the most important thing – my lunch!

Show day

This is the day you have been waiting for and you want to enjoy every minute. If you have chosen your events carefully and allowed yourself plenty of time, it should be a memorable and fun occasion.

Saturday evening
What an amazing day – my first show! I won two 3rds and a 6th, which were three rosettes more than I had hoped for. One of the 3rds was in the Working Hunter Pony class and the other two rosettes were for gymkhana events. Clever, clever Oscar!

At horse shows, there are often many classes taking place at the same time in separate rings. If you enter a lot of classes, you may find that two of them take place at the same time. You won't be able to get your entry money back if you have to miss a class. So take care when choosing which classes to enter. It is best to allow roughly an hour for each class. If you are entering a dressage competition, you will be allocated an exact time. You should present yourself to the dressage steward at least ten minutes beforehand.

Dressage

Show jumping

Lining up for the judge

Q How do I know when it is my turn to jump in a jumping class?

A The collecting ring is where you can warm up your pony before it is your turn to jump. The collecting ring steward sits at the entrance to the ring. He or she has a blackboard with the numbers of the competitors in the order that they will jump. You have to give your number to the steward. As competitors complete their round, the steward crosses out their numbers. Look at the blackboard, see which numbers are before you and be ready when those competitors enter the ring.

OUTSIDE THE RING

When you get to the show, visit the secretary's tent and collect your number. At a horse show, this will be a cardboard number that is worn round your waist. At a cross-country event, your number will be on a bib or tabard, so that it is displayed front and back. You will probably be asked for a deposit for this, which you'll get back when you return your number. When you are not actually taking part

in a class, make sure you don't tire out your pony or disturb other competitors and spectators by riding up and down the field.

Sunday

Before entering the jumping competition, I got some practice in the clear-round jumping. I paid an entry fee, did my round and would have won a clear-round rosette if Oscar hadn't knocked down the last pole. But it was good practice for the proper jumping competition.

Always remember to...

...smile at the judge if you are awarded a prize and say thank you when given your rosette. When everyone has been given their rosettes, you will be asked to do a lap of honour. This doesn't mean galloping madly round the arena. Instead, you should follow one another at a controlled canter. The winner usually does another lap of honour alone, while the others leave the arena.

THE TRAILER PARK

Your horse box or trailer should be parked so that there is enough room for your pony to be tied to the outside of it without interfering with the next horse box. If there is a long time between classes, you should give your pony a haynet. Your tack and grooming kit can be stored either inside or under the trailer. Make sure

they are somewhere where your pony cannot tread on them. It is best if someone can stay near the trailer all the time.

Don't leave your saddle on the ground where it could get damaged (above). Make sure your pony is happy before chatting to your friends (right).

After the show

Evening
We sang songs all the way home from the show. The ponies must have thought we were mad! I put Oscar in the stable and gave him some water (which he turned up his nose at) before his feed. He really enjoyed his food and it was dark by the time he finished. I thought I should leave him in tonight, but he was really keen to get into the field. He can have a rest tomorrow.

Whether you have a good day or a disastrous one, you and your pony will both be feeling very tired. It is important to take good care of your pony while you are still at the show and also once you are back at home.

1 Sweat scraper
Use this to remove any excess sweat. It is a useful tool to have, but not an essential one.

THE END OF THE DAY

When you have finished your classes, make sure your pony is comfortable. Remove the saddle, bridle and take out studs (see page 17). An unpicker is useful to take out the plaits. If your pony is very hot, cool it down with a sponge or stable rubber wrung out in cold water. Put on a summer sheet or rug. Leave your pony tied to the horse box and give it a haynet. Once you are ready to leave, put on your pony's travelling gear.

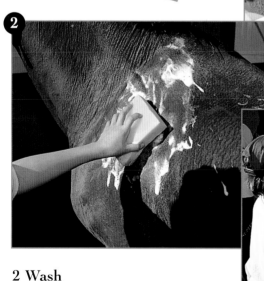

4 Turn out into the field
Ponies that live out should be let into their field after they've been fed and checked over.

2 Wash
After a cross-country round, your pony will be sweating hard and puffing. Use a sponge or an old tea towel to wipe over its body and legs with cold water.

3 Dry
Use an old towel to get rid of the water before putting on a sweat sheet.

CHECK YOUR PONY

Back at the stables, unload your pony from the horse box and take off its tail guard and travelling boots. If you haven't already done so, take out the plaits and brush out the mane and tail. In the stable, remove the rug and brush your pony with a body brush. Pay special attention to the legs. Pick out the hooves. Put on a night rug and give your pony water and a final feed. Hang up a haynet, then leave your pony in peace.

FINAL FEED

Your pony won't need more than its usual feed after a show. Extra feed can do more harm than good. Ponies that live out can be given their feed before being turned out. Offer fresh water first. Your pony will roll when you put it in the field. This is its way of relaxing.

Q What sort of injuries should I look for after the show?

A Your pony is unlikely to damage itself at an ordinary horse show, especially if it has done no more than take part in a showing class, a jumping class and a few gymkhana events. At a cross-country event, where you will have been jumping fixed fences, it is easy for your pony to knock itself. You should check its legs for any painful areas or cuts. Bad knocks will show up the next morning, so you should examine the legs for swelling and lumps. Treat minor cuts by bathing them gently in salted water. It is unlikely that there will be any serious injuries, but if there is anything you are unsure about, you must call your vet.

Monday
Dad made me a big notice board for my room. So far, it's only had photos of Oscar on it. But now it has my three rosettes. I've written details about the show on the back of the rosettes. Now I'll always know when Oscar and I won them and what we won them for.

Gymkhana events

Gymkhana games are likely to be your first taste of competition. Even if you need to be led on a leading rein, you can still take part. However, most events also require a lot of skill, fitness and riding ability, as you'll soon find out.

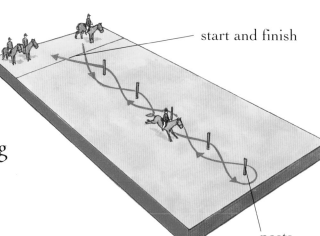

start and finish

posts

PRECISION GAMES

These games can involve balancing a ball on a cone or running along a line of stepping stones (right) without making a mistake. A steady, obedient pony will be more successful than a very fast one. It is best to concentrate on not making a mistake before trying to speed up.

SPEED GAMES

These are the games in which speed is more important than accuracy. In bending races, for example, each rider has to weave in and out of a line of oil drums or posts as quickly as possible. In most races you race against other riders. The races are not timed, so to win you must finish ahead of your rivals.

Lunchtime
Annabel and I are madly practising gymkhana games. It's more fun when we do it together and even better when other people join in.

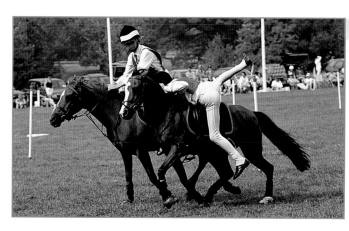

MIXED GAMES

These races combine precision and speed – racing to put a flag into a cone as quickly as possible, for example. All games need practice if you are to have success. You could join a Pony Club games squad to improve your technique.

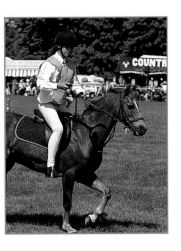

NECK-REINING

When you first start doing gymkhana games, you will find it difficult to control your pony without dropping equipment. What you need to do is to practise neck-reining. Hold the reins in one hand (usually the left) and move this hand across the withers. The pressure on your pony's neck tells it which way to go. Your other hand is then free to hold the equipment.

withers

Q How can I practise without the proper equipment?

A You can easily make or find gymkhana equipment. Buckets, tennis balls and old socks are easy to find. You can make an old sock bulkier by stuffing the toe with newspaper before rolling it up. For a flag, attach a piece of cloth to a bamboo pole. Half-fill an old detergent bottle with sand for practising the bottle race. Cones can be bought quite cheaply from builder's merchants. Bean poles make good bending poles. You may be able to buy them at a garden centre.

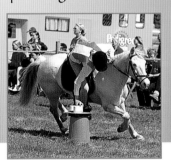

I did it! I did it! I actually managed to vault onto Oscar. The real secret is to keep Oscar moving at a brisk trot.

VAULTING

Some games call for the rider to get off to collect something before remounting and riding to the finish. Races are often lost by hopping round an excited pony, with one foot in the stirrup, trying to get on. Vaulting is something anyone can do, once the technique has been learned. It's worth spending some time practising.

Vaulting 2
Swing your right leg over the saddle. Use the hand on the saddle to steady yourself and the pony's forward movement to carry you up.

Direction of pony

Vaulting 1
Hold the reins and saddle as shown. Run beside your pony as it trots along. As the near fore foot (front foot nearest to you) hits the ground, push off with both feet and spring up.

The show ring

A showing class gives you the chance to display your pony and your riding skills. It will also let you see how your pony measures up against others. Here are a few things to remember when in a show ring.

Wednesday
I have decided that showing can be a bit boring. You spend a lot of time standing in a line doing nothing. Mind you, Oscar and I entered a Best Pony Club Pony showing event at the last show. It was good fun and we came 7th out of 42 entries. It was only our first time, so I was pretty pleased!

THE SALUTE

Riders salute to tell the judge they've finished their display. To do a salute, stand squarely in front of the judge. Hold the reins in your right hand and extend your other hand straight down (above right). Bow your head at the same time.

hard hat

beige or cream jodhpurs

tie worn with a white or pastel shirt

jacket, either tweed, black or navy blue

polished jodhpur boots

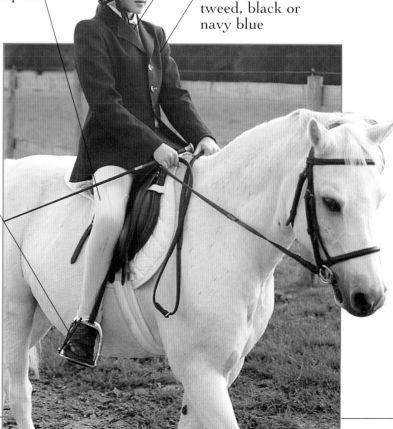

BEHAVIOUR IN THE SHOW RING

Ride round the ring at the same pace as the other riders. Leave one pony's length between you and the pony in front. Always make sure your pony looks its best, as you never know when the judge is looking at you.

Thursday

I picked up lots of schedules at the last show, so Annabel and I are having fun deciding which ones to go to. Next week, there's show jumping at the Old Oaks Equestrian Centre. There's even a pairs class, so the show seems just right for us.

YOUR PERSONAL SHOW

Your personal display is a chance to show your pony's paces. To do this, do a circuit of the ring at walk, trot and canter. Next, canter a figure-of-eight. Remember to slow down to a trot before you change the rein (direction). Halt by the judge, rein back (walk backwards) a few steps, salute and return to your place.

1 Warming up
You should allow at least half an hour to warm up your pony. This gets the stiffness out of its joints and helps it move easily.

2 The show
This is your chance to let the judge see how well-schooled and obedient your pony is. Try to be calm and confident.

STRIPPING OFF

If the judge wants to see your pony without its saddle, take off the saddle, numnah and martingale (if it wears one). Wait for your assistant to join you in the ring with a body brush and a stable rubber. Brush out the saddle mark. The judge will want to see your pony led away from and towards him or her. Make sure you take the reins over your pony's head to do this. You must also hold your pony steady while the judge examines it.

THE JUDGE

Your attitude towards the judge is something you develop in your first few shows. It's best not to argue with the judge's decision. All show judging is different and a lot depends on whether the judge likes your sort of pony. Always smile and thank the judge before you leave the ring.

15

Show jumping

This is the most popular of all competitive riding. It is available at many different levels and can be held inside or outside. It is enjoyed equally by novice and experienced riders. Most ponies and horses seem to enjoy it as much as their owners.

THE COURSE

Indoor show jumping usually has tricky, twisty courses in a small arena. Outdoor arenas usually have a free-flowing course with fewer sharp turns. All course designers try to build a course that will produce perhaps ten clear rounds, a jump-off against the clock and corners that can be cut.

finish

start

jump-off route

first-round route

Monday
I didn't really understand what unaffiliated jumping was. Then my instructor, Gerry, explained that it was for people like us whose ponies are not registered jumping ponies. In affiliated jumping, the rules are really strict. I think Oscar and I will stick to unaffiliated.

WALK THE COURSE

Never be tempted to skip this part of show jumping. Once you're in the ring, it's easy to lose your way. Walking the course helps you to remember where all the jumps are. It also gives

you an idea of any problems you might come across so that you can work out how to tackle them. In doubles (two jumps placed close together), pace out the distance between the two jumps. Then ask an experienced person to help you work out whether you should kick your pony on at one point, or let it take an extra stride between the two jumps.

Q How should I warm up for show jumping?

A As you get to know your pony, you will find out how much warming up it requires. If there is plenty of room at the show, it might be best to take your pony away from the other ponies. Do some quiet flatwork, such as walking, trotting and a few circles on both reins (both directions). Usually one or two practice jumps are set up in the collecting ring (the ring outside the jumping ring). Just before your round, it is worth popping your pony over these once or twice. Never spend too much time on practice jumps and don't make them too high.

THE JUMP SADDLE

If you do a lot of show jumping, it might be worth buying a special jumping saddle. It is designed to be used with shorter stirrup leathers and has a forward-cut saddle flap. This often has extra padding, called a knee roll. The seat tends to be shallower and the cantle lower than on a general purpose saddle. You will still need a general purpose saddle for hacking and other riding.

Always remember to...

...pack your studs. You may need them to give your pony extra grip if the competition is in an outside arena. Pointed studs are used on hard ground. Square, chunky studs are used when it's muddy. As well as studs, you need a T-tap for cleaning the stud-hole in the shoe. You'll also need a spanner for tightening the stud and petroleum jelly to lubricate the stud-hole before you put in the stud.

Don't forget to take out the studs as soon as the competition is over.

Petroleum jelly

Studs

T-tap

Evening
In a competition yesterday, there was a jump with trays of water under the poles. There were yellow plastic ducks floating in them! Oscar stood and stared at them for ages – we ended up being eliminated.

Sunday
Gerry gave us copies of a dressage test and told us to learn it. So Annabel and I marked out a dressage arena in the field and practised on foot until we really knew the test. Now let's see how Oscar manages!

Dressage

There is nothing mystical about dressage. It is just a way of training your horse or pony to carry out basic movements fluently, calmly and obediently. Any type of pony will improve with schooling, and a well-schooled pony is a pleasure to ride.

K   E   H

A   C

The dressage arena
A standard arena is 40 by 20 metres and you can mark it out on any flat piece of ground. You can paint the letters on cones or old paint cans. Place them as shown here. The letters K, H, M and F should be six metres from the corners on the long sides. In a dressage test, the rider always enters at A. The centre of the arena is known as X.

F   B   M

DRESSAGE SADDLE

This saddle isn't very comfortable for everyday riding, but it does get you into the correct position for dressage. It has a very deep seat and a straight-cut flap. The girth straps hanging below the panel show that it is meant to be used with a short girth. This stops the girth buckle from lying under your thigh.

CLOTHING FOR DRESSAGE

For dressage you should be clean and tidy, just as you are for showing. You should also wear gloves. Spurs and a whip are allowed. Your pony should also be well-groomed with its mane plaited. Make sure your pony isn't wearing any boots, bandages, a saddle cloth, a coloured browband or anything else fancy. Don't be afraid to ask the organiser of a dressage competition if you are unsure of the dress rules.

A K E H F B M C

Collected walk

Working trot

DRESSAGE TESTS

Dressage tests usually last about five minutes. They include different movements and paces for you and your pony to perform in a particular order. You have to do several changes of pace and direction. You can get a copy of the test from the event organiser. Dressage tests are specially written for dressage competitions and for the dressage section of a one-day event.

I got my first dressage score sheet back. It wasn't great, but the comments were very helpful. I'll do better next time.

Extended trot

Medium canter

Q How is dressage scored?

A All dressage tests are divided into sections. Each section contains one or more movements, such as a change of rein. You are given marks out of 10 for each section. A score of 5 or more is a passing grade. These marks are recorded on your score sheet, along with any comments the judge makes. Marks are also given for the overall performance of both you and your pony. In a dressage competition, the competitor with the highest mark is the winner. In combined training (dressage and show jumping) and one-day events, the final mark is the number of penalties given. Penalties are given for any mistakes you make. So in these cases, the lower the score the better.

DRESSAGE PACES

All of the movements that you do at junior level dressage are relatively easy for the average horse or pony. The paces are simply what you would normally do in basic schooling. When riding your test, try to concentrate on accuracy, smooth transitions from one pace to another and getting your pony to bend when turning a circle. In many competitions you will be expected to perform the test from memory.

One-day event

This is a very popular event and is a true test of your pony's all-round ability. It combines the discipline of dressage, the stamina of cross-country jumping and the accuracy and timing of the show jumping ring. It is organised at all levels, from novice to experienced.

My first one-day event was a DISASTER. I fell off on the cross-country course and then went the wrong side of a flag!

DRESSAGE

This is always the first of the three parts of a one-day event. The score that you get is the dressage penalty score. So you want it to be as low as possible.

SHOW JUMPING

This takes place before or after the cross-country. It is an ordinary show jumping course. Any penalties that you get are added to the dressage score.

Stream

Tyres

Tiger trap

Finish

Start

Coffin

CHECKING THE COURSE

A plan of the cross-country course is always displayed. Study it carefully bef your turn. The time allowed to compl the course is also given and you will g time penalties if you exceed it.

V-shaped jump with alternative routes

WATER JUMPS

Only experienced riders have to jump into or out of water, but you might be asked to splash through water and perhaps jump a fence at the other side. If your pony hates water, some courses provide a learner fence to jump instead of going through the water.

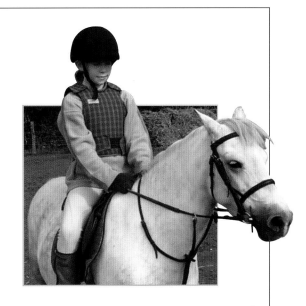

BODY PROTECTORS

All cross-country riders should wear body protectors. These are specially designed, padded tabards that absorb shock and protect your spine, ribs and shoulders. You should have your body protector properly fitted by a trained supplier.

Straw bales

Bench or chair

Trakehner

THE CROSS-COUNTRY COURSE

Each jump is clearly numbered and is flagged with red and white flags. You ride between the flags. The red flag must be on your right and the white one on your left. Some jumps have more than one route. The shorter, direct route is often much more difficult.

Puzzle with alternative routes

Always remember to...

...plan the timing of your cross-country ride carefully. As you walk the course, note the places where you have to go slowly because of difficult ground. Just as importantly, note the places where you are able to speed up. This will help you to know where to make up some time if you feel that you are falling behind. Look carefully at each jump. In particular, decide which route you are going to take on those jumps that have more than one route. Does your pony like water? If not, then look to see whether or not there is a learner fence you can jump instead.

Transportation

Not many riders hack to shows because of the amount of traffic on the roads. Once you start competing regularly, you will need to use a trailer or horse box. This gives you the chance to take part in different events over interesting and varied courses.

TRAVEL PROTECTION

Travel clothing guards against knocks and keeps your pony clean for the show. Ponies usually wear travelling boots when being transported in a trailer. These go from above the knee to just above the hoof. Your pony should also wear a lightweight rug, a tail bandage and a tail guard. If your pony throws its head up a lot, it is a good idea for it to wear a poll guard on top of its head.

tail bandage

rug

travelling boots

4 pm – I think Oscar must have been fed in a trailer when he was young because I never have any problem loading him. In fact, twice he has walked into the trailer on his own while I was talking to Annabel!

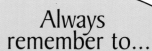

Always remember to...

...clean the trailer after you have used it. If the floor is wet, remove any straw and leave the ramps down so that air can circulate and allow the floor to dry. It is most important for your pony's safety that the floor should not rot. Cleaning and drying it should prevent this. Don't clean out your trailer while you are still at the show – it is very annoying for the owner of the field.

THE TRAILER

A two-horse trailer is the most popular kind of
trailer as it lets your pony travel with a companion.
Trailers with a front and a rear ramp are good,
as your pony doesn't have to be backed out. This
can make it less frightening for a nervous pony.
Always load your pony by calmly walking in
a straight line up the ramp. Tie up your pony
with quite a short length of rope.

trailer

trailer
ramp

stall

partition

THE WRONG WAY

Never try to load your
pony as shown here. Your
pony will win a battle like
this because it is stronger
than you. If your pony is
difficult to load, ask an
experienced person for help.

Q What do I need to know about hacking to
a show?

A If the route is a safe one and you do not
have big roads to cross or to ride along,
hacking can be fun. Plan your route beforehand
so that you know exactly which way to go.
Take a head-collar with you, either on your
pony or buckled round your waist. Allow
plenty of time and enjoy the trip. It is best
to travel with friends. At the showground,
find a shady spot where you can tie up
your pony. It helps if someone else can bring
things like your grooming kit in the car.

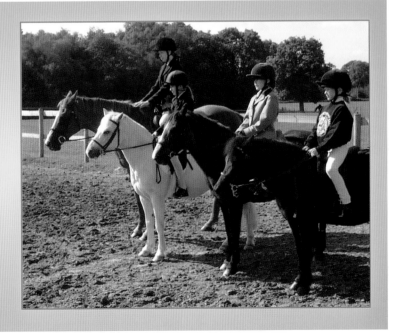

Extra schooling

Evening – At our stables, Gerry is always around to help when things go wrong. Recently, Oscar started running out to the right when I was jumping. I didn't know why so I asked Gerry to watch me in the school. Apparently I was pulling the right rein without even realising it.

There is nothing like a competition for showing up basic problems, either yours or your pony's. Either way, there is only one answer – you both have to go back to school. If possible, get a good instructor to help you smooth out the rough patches.

TAKING DEFEAT
Losing is hard to take. The most important thing to do is to accept defeat gracefully. Go away, do some schooling and come back to do your best at the next show. Remember that entering competitions is all about enjoying yourself. It isn't just the winning that is important.

GRID WORK
Getting back to basics is a good way to improve your chances at the next show. If your pony is rushing its jumps and not following your commands, however hard you try, you need to go back to the very beginning. Walk your pony calmly over poles on the ground. Then progress slowly to a grid of small jumps. Don't try to advance too quickly or all the old problems will come back. It is important to get your pony going steadily for you, answering to your legs and voice. Soon you will be able to complete a course of jumps without any problems.

Make a video
One of the most helpful ways of improving your riding is to get a friend to video you during a schooling session. Until you see yourself riding, it can be difficult to tell just what you are doing wrong.

BAD POSITION

It is important to keep a contact with your pony's mouth through the reins. This rider (near right) has reins that are too long. He has little control of his pony. The other rider (far right) is being left behind as the pony goes over the jump. Help your pony by sitting in the correct position and giving clear instructions.

Jumping too early

Oscar is turning into a really good jumper. I think he is enjoying it, as his ears always prick up when we enter the ring.

JUMPING PROBLEMS

Both the problems illustrated here show that you need to help your pony know when to take off. In the first, the pony has taken off too soon and will need to stretch out too far to clear the jump. In the second, a late take-off means the pony knocks the jump down. With practice you can learn to recognise your pony's stride and when it should take off.

Jumping too late

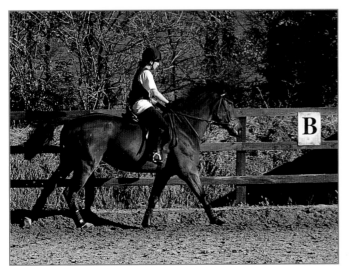

FLATWORK

Flatwork is the most important part of training. By doing flatwork you will be able to do more exciting activities, like jumping, more efficiently, safely and successfully. Try to spend a short time each day on schooling on the flat until your pony is stepping out confidently. As you improve, gradually introduce more advanced movements. Make sure you keep having lessons with an experienced instructor.

Unusual activities

There are many different types of competition to enter and lots of ways to enjoy your pony. Here are some of the fun things that you can take part in. If you ask around, you may be able to join a group or club in your area.

Cross-country riding

Tuesday
Annabel and I had an invitation to learn all about tetrathlon. We were given a chance to shoot and shown exactly how to stand and hold the pistol. I completely missed the target with my first shot, but I soon learned not to wait too long before lining up and firing. I think it's another thing that you just get better and better at with practice!

TETRATHLON

This is a four-part event organised by the Pony Club. The competition usually takes place over two days. It creates a great feeling of team spirit and you are likely to make many friends. The four parts include riding over a cross-country course, shooting with a .177 air pistol, cross-country running over a certain distance and swimming as far as you can in a certain number of minutes. The older you are, the further or longer the races will be. Usually, the shooting and swimming are held on the first day and riding and running are held on the second. The points you get for each event are added together to find the winner.

Race information

- Riding – 1600-2500 m cross-country

- Running – 1000-3000 m

- Swimming – points are scored for every metre swum for 2-3 minutes

- Shooting – 10 shots at two targets from 7-10 m

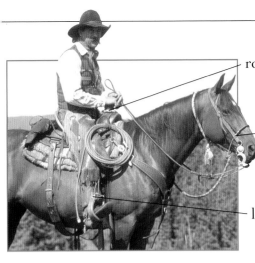

roping horn

Western bridle

long leather stirrups

WESTERN RIDING

Western riders use a specially designed saddle and bridle. A Western saddle has a roping horn, a high cantle and long leather stirrups. It is heavier than an ordinary saddle and the horse is gradually introduced to it. You sit deep in the saddle and ride with long stirrup leathers. This allows you to sit in the saddle for a long time without getting too tired. This is useful for cowboys who spend many hours in the saddle. You hold the reins with one hand and use neck-reining to steer the horse.

Lunchtime
I thought I might take up endurance riding and went for a really long three-hour ride. Oscar was fine when we got back, but I was so exhausted I could hardly stand. Perhaps endurance riding can wait!

ENDURANCE RIDING

Endurance riding is competing over long distances to be completed as efficiently as possible without distress to your pony. At various points along the route, your pony is examined by a vet before you're allowed to continue. You are also met by an assistant who gives you and your pony whatever help or refreshment you need.

Q What is the difference between the tetrathlon and the modern pentathlon?

A The modern pentathlon consists of riding, shooting, running, swimming and fencing. The tetrathlon doesn't include fencing. Most pentathletes start their career in the Pony Club and then take up fencing as they get older. Riding in modern pentathlon is different from tetrathlon because the competitors ride horses that they have never seen before. The riding is usually over a show-jumping course. In tetrathlon, you ride your own pony and you don't do any show jumping. In ordinary athletics, the pentathlon comprises various field and track events and dates back to as long ago as 708 BC.

Polo

Some horse activities, like polo, go back several centuries or even longer. Others have only been around for a few years. If you ask around, you will find out about many new, exciting things to try, some more difficult than others.

Saturday
Someone asked me if I'd like to join the polo squad, so I went to watch a practice. It looked fun. The problem is, if I played polo, I wouldn't have time to do much else. Also, you usually have to travel a long way to play in a polo tournament. I'd definitely like to give it a try one day though.

ORIGINS OF POLO
Polo was played as long ago as 500 BC. It began in Central Asia and became popular in China by the 700s AD. The British discovered polo in India around 1850 and it later crossed the Atlantic to America.

goal line

side line

goal posts

40 yard mark

safety zone

starting point

THE GAME
The aim is to hit the ball through your opponents' goal. There are two teams, each with four members. At junior level, games consist of one or two six-minute periods, known as chukkas.

POLOCROSSE

This is a mixture of polo and lacrosse. It's played with special sticks that can scoop up the foam rubber ball. There are six players to a team, but only three are on the field at any one time. Each half of the team plays alternate chukkas. There are between two and eight chukkas in a match. A player is only allowed to ride one pony in a match.

Always remember to...

...have the welfare of your pony in mind. In polo, although a chukka is only six minutes long, the game is fast and furious. This can put a strain on your pony's joints. You can protect your pony's legs from accidental knocks by using boots and knee pads, but the twists and turns can cause damage. So make sure that your pony gets enough rest between chukkas.

HORSEBALL

In horseball, a goal is scored when the ball is thrown through a net similar to the one used in basketball. The ball is about the size of a football and has leather hand grips on it to make it easier to hold. A goal cannot be scored until all four members of the team have held the ball.

VAULTING

This is a form of gymnastics on horseback. The best type of horse has a broad back and smooth paces. Usually, the horse wears a numnah fitted with a roller bar, instead of a saddle. The rider performs various acrobatics while the horse canters round the arena. In some displays, more than one athlete will take part in exercises on one horse. Apart from having a well-trained horse, the rider needs to be very fit and athletic.

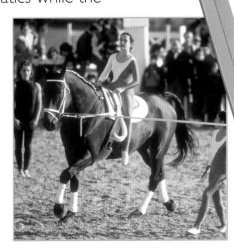

2 pm – I think I could get quite interested in polocrosse. There is a group near my house who plays polocrosse, so I could try it if I wanted. Oh dear! There are so many things Oscar and I could do, there just aren't enough hours in the day.

Quiz Time

Can you remember what you have learned in this book? Why not test yourself and your friends by taking this quiz.

1 What is useful for making your pony's white socks look whiter?

2 What does a collecting ring steward do in a jumping competition?

3 Why is neck-reining useful in gymkhana games?

4 How much room should you leave between you and the pony in front when riding round a show ring?

5 How big is a standard dressage arena?

6 Starting with A and moving clockwise round the dressage arena, write down the letters in their correct order.

7 In a cross-country competition, which coloured flag should be on your right?

8 Which events make up the tetrathlon?

9 What is the term given to the period of play in polo?

Useful addresses

The Pony Club
The Pony Club HQ
NAC
Stoneleigh Park
Kenilworth
Warwickshire
CV8 2RW
Tel: 01327 361 388
www.pony-club.org.uk

Association of British
Riding Schools
Queens Chambers
38–40 Queen Buildings
Queen Street
Penzance
Cornwall
TR18 4HB
Tel: 01736 69440

Thursday
I'm really getting the hang of entering shows now. It's good to know what to expect each time – I can enjoy myself even more!

Answers
1 Chalk. 2 He or she takes the competitor's number, marks the order of jumping and makes sure the riders are ready for their turn. 3 It leaves you one hand free for holding equipment. 4 At least one pony's length. 5 40 metres by 20 metres. 6 A, K, E, H, C, M, B, F. 7 The red flag. 8 Shooting, swimming, running and riding. 9 Chukka.

Glossary

bending race
Gymkhana game in which competitors weave through a row of poles.

body protector
Specially padded garment worn to protect a rider in a fall.

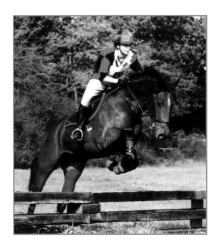

chukka
Period of play in polo and polocrosse.

class
Each show is split into classes. You choose which classes to enter. Different classes are designed to cater for different abilities and age groups.

collecting ring
Area at the entrance to a showing or jumping ring where competitors gather.

dressage test
Set of movements to be performed by each rider in a dressage competition.

figure-of-eight
Movement performed in shape of an eight to demonstrate a horse's agility.

hunter trials
Cross-country competition.

knee roll
Padded area at the front of the saddle flap on a jumping saddle.

neat's foot oil
Substance that can be painted onto leather to keep it supple.

neck-reining
Guiding the pony with only one hand on the reins.

pentathlon
Five-part competition including shooting, swimming, running, riding and fencing.

poll guard
Protection for the part of a pony's head between its ears.

polo
Game played on horseback with mallet-shaped sticks.

salute
Gesture made by a rider to tell the judge that they have finished their display.

schedule
List of classes in a show or cross-country event.

stripping off
Taking off your pony's saddle so that the show judge can see the shape of your pony.

tetrathlon
Four-part competition consisting of shooting, swimming, running and riding.

travelling boots
Padded leggings that stretch from above the pony's knee to the hoof, used when travelling.

T-tap
Spanner used for cleaning stud holes and tightening studs.

vaulting
1) Gymnastics on horseback.
2) Leaping onto a pony, particularly in mounted games.

walking the course
Going on foot round a show jumping or cross-country course.

Index

Photo credits
Abbreviations: l-left, r-right, b-bottom, t-top, c-centre, m-middle
Front and back cover, 1, 4tr, 5bl, 5br, 6mr all, 7ml, 7br, 8c, 9bm, 10br, 11c, 14tr both, 16mr, 18bm, 21tl, 21tr, 22 both, 23 all, 24c, 25bl, 26tr, 30tl, 31ml, 32bl – Select Pictures. 3b, 9br, 16ml, 20ml, 20c, 27tl, 27bm, 28br, 29bm, 32tr – Corel. 4c, 5c, 8t, 12c, 13tl, 13c, 15br, 24bl, 27ml, 29mr – Horsepix. 4br, 7tr all, 8mr, 9tl, 9bl, 10c, 10bm, 10bl, 11t, 12br, 15ml, 15c, 16ml, 20b, 29ml – Kit Houghton Photography. 6ml, 14br, 24br – Aubrey Wade.